DEVOTED

— TO —

HIM

— FOR —

THEM

ENCOURAGEMENT FOR THOSE
WHO *Serve* OTHERS

DEVOTED

— TO —

HIM

—— for ——

THEM

ENCOURAGEMENT FOR THOSE
WHO *Serve* OTHERS

CHERYL RILEY

Copyright © 2019 by Cheryl Riley
Library of Congress Cataloguing-in-Publication Data
TXu002120253

Devoted to Him for Them
Encouragement for Those Who Serve Others
ISBN # 978-0-692-19604-5

Cover design by Derick Harris
Published by Blesspatt Books
Charlotte, NC – USA
www.CherylCRiley.com
Facebook/Devoted to Him for Them

Dedication

This book is dedicated to all the children we, as educators, have had the privilege of molding, guiding, shaping and instructing over the years. May the seeds we planted in your lives continue to germinate, grow and blossom as you strive to reach God's fullest potential for your lives.

Foreword

I am honored and delighted to write the foreword to this outstanding devotional designed to encourage, motivate and challenge educators on every level. As children are at the heart of God, it's evident that our Heavenly Father orchestrated this devotional to reach the hearts of all administrators and teachers.

Mrs. Cheryl Riley was one of our first teachers hired when we began our Christian school in 1989. As her pastor since that time, I have watched her blossom as a Christian, wife, mother and teacher, and it has been a joy. Before our first principal of 27 years retired, God had been grooming Cheryl, over the years, to serve in that position. In retrospect, only God knew His plans for her would include stepping into the Head Master's role in which she has done an outstanding job.

This daily devotional is full of the Word of God, personal experiences and transparency that will cause every reader to be drawn closer to God and to examine their hearts, attitudes and commitment to children or to others they may serve. As you read, there will be times of laughter and appreciation for the goodness and mercy of God.

May I, in all sincerity, ask that you approach each of the 31-daily devotionals with a humble heart expecting the Holy Spirit to speak to you? This is an inspirational workbook that prompts us to think about our interactions with others, honestly assess ourselves and recognize God's instructions to help us excel in life.

In closing, I also recommend this book to every parent as it will enrich their lives and relationship with their children. I'm grateful that Cheryl followed the Lord's leading in putting her heart in print. This devotional is truly a blessing!

Pastor Robyn Gool
Victory Christian Center
Charlotte, NC

Acknowledgements

This work has been more than 10 years in the making. I am so grateful for those who have encouraged me along the way. I am especially grateful for my husband, Alvin Riley, and for all his loving support. I could not have completed this project without his prayers, encouragement, candid input and unequivocal guidance. Thanks for being such a godly role model for our children and the backbone of our family. With all my heart, I appreciate the sacrifices you make, and I love you dearly.

I am thankful for my three children who have been my 24/7 pupils. You all have been my staying power. As I look at each of you, I know that giving up was never an option.

To my bestie, Phyllis, who has pumped and pushed me at every turn, I believe your prophecies. To my coach, Melissa, who has repeatedly stirred the nest and nudged me toward the birth of this work, thank you. To Rose, whose idea helped inspire me to write this devotional, thank you for seeing what I didn't know was there. To my partner in the work, Joi, thank you for finishing my sentences, reading my mind and showing humble sensitivity to the Lord and His Word. To Carol, my 5 a.m. wake-up call, 30 years later, we remain committed to "cutting on the sun." Thanks for being my stabilizer. To LeNette, thank you for bringing me along on your journey. You're right; it's time to act on all that we have learned and been exposed to. Finally, I thank God for my pastor, Robyn Gool, and his wife, Marilyn, being an example of faithfulness and commitment to the vision God has placed on the inside of you. It has been my pleasure to serve God under your leadership.

INTRODUCTION

From an early age, my career goals were fueled by one ambition which was simply to make lots of money. That's why when I heard my church was looking for teachers to start a Christian school, the announcement flew in one ear and out the other. I knew it didn't apply to me, because teachers didn't make any money. Besides, I was holding out for a high-paying more aristocratic career. Since I was a child, I dreamt of becoming a successful lawyer, but my intrigue with problem-solving led to a college major in math and minor in computer science. But as I was in the lab typing my senior exit paper, a freshman named Larry came in asking how to solve a simple math problem. Having been a college tutor for four years, I stopped to explain it to him. Although reviewing steps to resolve the math problem -150/10 should have taken a few minutes at the most, it took me at least 30 minutes to get it to click for him.

Not only was I determined to help him get it, but I patiently waited rehashing the steps until he did. Yet, still I saw no connection between my teaching and tutoring background and a barely-paying school teaching job. Somehow, I had even dismissed the fact that I had been teaching Sunday School since I was 13. Nonetheless, by the time I returned to church, the announcement about teaching positions had discontinued, so I assumed they were all filled; yet, I wasn't disappointed. But in my spirit, I felt an urging to submit a resume. To my surprise, I was called in for three interviews, and 30 years later, I'm still here. That's after 25 years as a math teacher, two years as assistant principal and now in my third year as principal.

Over the years as I reminisced about various classroom scenarios, it occurred to me that while I was teaching the children, they were actually teaching me. I learned instructing children is a selfless role that centers around giving rather than getting. Somehow, working with children stimulates an insatiable desire within you to want to help every child succeed. Although successes are not measured monetarily in my field, I'm still enjoying the recidivism from seeds sown decades after students are grown and on their own. Ironically, the greater children's needs, the more compelled I feel to fix them, and for 30 years that has fueled my desire to keep coming back every day and every year.

You'll see exactly what I mean as you embrace the inspirational lessons in these 30 very real-life devotionals. As you see yourself in them, they will brighten your perspective, and you'll certainly enjoy a few good laughs. This book not only provides you alternatives for overcoming obstacles at work and in your personal life, it also shows you how to get the most out of them while cultivating diamonds in the rough regardless of their shapes, sizes or pedigrees.

Day 1

Energize Your Class Environment

Scripture:

"Whoever welcomes one of these little children in my name welcomes me; and whoever welcomes me does not welcome me but the one who sent me."
~ *Mark 9:37 (NIV)*

"Whoever welcomes a prophet as a prophet will receive a prophet's reward, and whoever welcomes a righteous person as a righteous person will receive a righteous person's reward."
~ *Matthew 10:41 (NIV)*

For faculty and staff, beginning a new school year is like finding or building a new home for your family. As we begin our new year, we must think of it as an opportunity to showcase our homes. Whenever new subdivisions open, the builder does his best to entice new homeowners to move into his community. He does so by developing immaculate landscaping with decorative flowers to enhance the entryways and tastefully-designed furnishings to appeal to a broad spectrum of visitors.

Upon arriving in search of the perfect home, prospective homeowners are cordially greeted by an engaging sales agent who knowledgeably shares all the wonderful amenities and benefits of the new subdivision. As a result of the builder's thoughtful planning for his customers, potential buyers are so wowed by the well-packaged presentation that they eagerly place bids or sign contracts. They're convinced the house is just what they're looking for. Although unsure of what utilities would cost or who their new neighbors might be, they are willing to take a chance because the environment is warm, orderly and inviting and the atmosphere feels just like home.

The above scenario summarizes our mission. As we prepare for the arrival of our students, we want to use our imaginations to create aesthetically pleasing environments. Surroundings that say, "Welcome. Please come on in, and make yourself comfortable." We want our work environments (classrooms, labs, cafeteria, library) to radiate a spirit of love and peace in which parents can safely trust and students can learn and explore with hearts of excitement and adventure.

Prayer:

Heavenly Father,

I thank You for helping me to create a welcoming classroom that is safe and inviting for my students, parents and visitors. I thank You that this is a place they long to come to and hate to leave.

Reflection:

What are my students/parents saying about my room?

_____

_____

_____

_____

_____

_____

_____

Is this the response I was expecting to receive? If not, how will I adjust to the feedback?

_____

_____

_____

_____

_____

Day 2

They Believe That
I Believe in them

Scripture:

"I can do all things through Christ who strengthens me." ~ Philippians 4:13 (NKJV)

YES you Can! During the 2008 Presidential election, then candidate Senator Barack Obama galvanized the nation around the slogan, "Yes We Can!" His campaign motto became even more popular after singer Will.i.am wrote a song with that title featuring Mr. Obama. Watched by more than 22 million viewers on YouTube, this song helped ignite supporters around the Obama campaign, and he won the nomination and ultimately the presidency. How? Why? Mr. Obama clearly stated his belief in the American people, convincing them that under his leadership, they too could win. And his campaign slogan, "Yes We Can," became a reality.

Isn't it also our mission to share with our students our desires and aspirations for them? Shouldn't we continuously energize them by repeatedly confessing God's word over them and assuring them of our commitment to their success? These are great components for obtaining student and parent buy-in which leads to a strong team working in unison toward a common goal. Likewise, our assignment also involves convincing students that negative circumstances, statements, actions or thoughts will remain in the past and will in no way

hinder our perceptions of them, or their opportunities
to go forward because we believe in them.

Heavenly Father,

*I thank You that our school is a haven of hope for
our students. They are free to take risks without fear
of judgment. This school is an incubator full of
endless possibilities for our children to achieve and
see their goals and dreams realized.*

Reflection:

How do I show that I believe in those I serve?

_____

_____

_____

_____

_____

_____

_____

_____

_____

What are students or others saying when I am not in the room?

_____

_____

_____

_____

_____

_____

_____

_____

_____

Day 3

Fly Butterfly Fly

Scripture:

"For I know the thoughts that I think toward you, saith the LORD, thoughts of peace, and not of evil, to give you an expected end." ~ Jeremiah 29:11 (KJV)

"The steps of a good man are ordered by the LORD: and he delighteth in his way." ~ Psalm 37:23 (KJV)

The fall of 2011 was a turning point for my family. Our oldest, who had been working for a prominent bank in New York City's financial district, was informed that her contract was not being renewed although she had just received a positive evaluation. After dealing with a series of sports injuries, our oldest son decided during his senior year of college to forgo his final year of eligibility on his football scholarship, so he could focus on his studies and graduate in the spring. Although he had met all course requirements, he had no employment prospects. And our youngest decided he was changing his major to history and education rather than follow his dad, brother and sister in the business arena.

This was truly a time of uncertainty; neither of our children had a clear view of what the future held. This was a time of change. As I began to reflect on their plight, I thought of a caterpillar entering a cocoon. While in this closed environment, he is in a place of struggle. The struggle is work which is frustrating and must be endured alone. If you attempted to assist him in the process, it could prove detrimental. I am sure you can imagine how I, as a mother, wanted to fix their problems for them. But this was a time of transformation and growth for each of them. They needed to know that there was an answer and that answer was found in quietness in their Father's cocoon.

They all sought Him and He answered them. Our daughter landed a new position and skillset, leadership experience, traveled the world and is currently working on her MBA. The football player accepted one of several business opportunities offered him and has transitioned to a different company and been promoted with a substantial raise in record time. That business convert is now teaching and serving as grade level chair and was named teacher of the year for the department during his first year. He is a published author and has sat on several panels as a voice for educators.

Unexpected change can be good. Although uncomfortable, it pushes us toward the plans God has for our lives. The same way the caterpillar emerges from its place, transforms and then develops its wings, God expects us to reach our full potential. *Fly Butterfly Fly!*

Prayer:

Heavenly Father,

I thank You for ordering the steps of each student. I thank You that they are able to expect and embrace change knowing that Your plans for them are good. In Jesus' name. Amen.

Reflection:

How do I face my cocoon.....transition?

_____

_____

_____

_____

In what ways am I trusting God to give me wings?

_____

_____

_____

_____

_____

Day 4

Who Did You Ask?

Scripture:

"And I say unto you, Ask, and it shall be given you; seek, and ye shall find; knock, and it shall be opened unto you! For every one that asketh receiveth; and he that seeketh findeth; and to him that knocketh it shall be opened." ~ Luke 11:9-10 (KJV)

It is so easy to tell why something cannot be done. An excuse can be made for everything and anything that we wish to give one for. So, you told me why it cannot be done... But who have you gone to for assistance? Many times, we remain stagnant because we have not reached out. Did we ask God for help? Or did we ask a teacher, a colleague or supervisor?

Sometimes, being the new Kid (teacher) on the block or the youngest one in the group can be intimidating. Perhaps, you've been around for years and feel asking questions somehow diminishes you. Wrong thoughts, wrong voice. Just as we share with our children, we must remember everyone needs help at some time or other, and it's okay to receive help.

Not asking pertinent questions can leave us in a quandary of wrong decisions, wasted time and money and even the loss of valuable relationships; when all we had to do was ask.

Prayer:

Heavenly Father,

Thank You for being my ever-present help. I receive Your guidance and direction, and I thank You for leading me to those who have the services and resources I need. I resist pride and submit myself to You and to them to fulfill Your plan for me. In Jesus' name. Amen.

Reflection:

What's keeping me from asking questions?

_____

_____

_____

_____

_____

_____

_____

Day 5

Are You Still in the Same Spot?

Scripture:

"He has filled them with skill to do all kinds of work as engravers, designers, embroiderers in blue, purple and scarlet yarn and fine linen, and weavers – all of them skilled workers and designers."
~ *Exodus 35:35 (NIV)*

Engaging the attention of those you instruct is not a luxury but a necessity. In order for your audience to receive from you, they must be engaged. Traditional teaching often depicted teachers standing before a classroom of tiny humans; dispensing information in hopes of them receiving, understanding and later regurgitating exactly what was shared with little deviation. For many students these are delusional expectations. The days of 'sit and get' are long gone. In the words of Marcia Tate, *"Worksheets Don't Grow Dendrites."*

We've got to make connections. We must employ the use of stations, technology, voice inflection and dramatization to reach them. Otherwise, we're no more effective than Charlie Brown's teacher whose voice was merely noisy musical chords to "Wong, wong, wong."

We must move and engage them to make learning memorable. Think of how you feel during faculty meetings or professional development activities. Those same thoughts are going through the minds and from the lips of your students about you. Become what you wish your presenters would be.

Prayer:

Heavenly Father,

Thank You for equipping me to reach and engage all learners. Lead me to resources, websites, courses and individuals that will develop and stretch me to do the same in them. I receive creative ideas and insight on best practices and lesson delivery. With your help my class is engaging and enriching. In Jesus' Name. Amen.

What ingredients are missing in my classroom?

_____

_____

_____

Day 6

Jake from State Farm

Scripture:

"A merry heart doeth good like a medicine: but a broken spirit drieth the bones."
~ Proverbs 17:22 (KJV)

During my first year as a principal, a teacher sent a child to the office to address disrespectful behavior... talking without permission and talking back. In the middle of the lesson, the teacher heard continual talking and asked, "Who said that?" The student responded with a tag line from a popular commercial. "Jake from State Farm."

Now, I am not sure if you've ever seen the commercial, but it shows a man downstairs talking on the phone during the wee hours of the night when his wife enters wondering who has lured him from the comforts of their bed to converse at that hour. As the husband talks with a telemarketer, he responds to her, "It's Jake....from State Farm." Having seen the commercial, I recognized the line.

After having the student explain her comment, my office colleague and I locked eyes and did our best to avoid doubling over in laughter. We actually found the response ingenious and funny, but I couldn't let the student know that since she used it inappropriately. Because she had been sent to me for correction, I couldn't let her return to class thinking it was okay to disrespect those in authority. So, I asked her, "Have you ever seen or heard a comedian?" She said she had, and I responded, "Well, when teaching, we must respect the person with the microphone. He or she is going to have the last word. In other words, respect the mic."

As I pondered this scenario, I thought about how important it is for us to applaud the talents of our students. To diffuse the situation in our classroom, a good alternative response may have been: "That was pretty good. I'll give you that one; I like that commercial too. Now turn in your books to pages…"

Not every supposedly negative response is a discipline issue. Some behaviors truly identify students' giftings, and part of our role as teachers is finding and cultivating those gifts. That particular student is very witty and bright, and just a few days later, she used conversation to command the attention of a whole classroom. It's okay to laugh at their jokes even when they're on us. There are always teachable moments.

Prayer:

Heavenly Father,

Thank You for helping me to loosen up and laugh at myself. Help me to avoid unnecessary disciplinary actions. Enable me to see the gifts in each of my students. Help me to create a world in which the children want to dwell.

Reflection:

How comfortable are students in my classroom? Why are some students comfortable and others uncomfortable?

_____

_____

_____

_____

_____

How am I recognizing their gifts and steering them in the direction of those gifts?

_____

_____

_____

_____

_____

_____

Day 7

Shut Up!

Scripture:

"Let your speech be always with grace, seasoned with salt, that ye may know how ye ought to answer every man." ~ Colossians 4:6 (KJV)

"So Samuel said, 'When you were little in your own eyes, were you not head of the tribes of Israel? And did not the LORD anoint you king over Israel?'" ~ I Samuel 15:17 (NKJV)

"Therefore humble yourselves under the mighty hand of God, that He may exalt you in due time." ~ I Peter 5:6 (NKJV)

Shut up is such an ugly phrase, teachers shouldn't use it toward students...unless students completely disregard several advance warnings.☺ Or at least that's how I felt one morning during devotions. Our school day begins with devotions and a Bible lesson. Prior to the lesson, students recite in unison pledges (to the American flag, the Christian flag and the Bible). After patriotic, praise and worship songs are sung, we end with prayer.

One morning, I repeatedly reminded the whole class that devotions were a sacred time and should be respected. Well, you guessed it. After three "Please get quiet" appeals, and two "No talking during devotions" warnings, I belted out "SHUT UP!" The class understood and quickly got in line, except for one young lady who began mumbling under her breath.

That was not a good idea. I called her name and asked if she was talking and why? She replied, "Ain't nobody talking to you." At this point, I was ready to take my earrings off and *take her on*... but wisdom overrode my emotions, so I said nothing. At the end of class, I asked if I could speak with her. "What was that all about?" I asked. "Why did you respond to me in that manner?" Her response was, "Why did you yell SHUT UP?" "Ouch!" I immediately apologized, explaining to her that she was correct; I had been a poor example. I asked if she would please forgive me, which she did, and she apologized as well.

Although the children's behavior was not appropriate, it was not okay for me to use degrading behavior. Correction was warranted, but my method was improper. We must be quick to admit when we are wrong and be quick to apologize. Transparency breeds authentic relationships between teachers and students. Students will in turn recognize our willingness to hear and understand them. Since we're all humans capable of mistakes, when we mess up, we should own up.

Prayer:

Heavenly Father,

Help me to see the children as You do and to respect the gifts that stand/sit before me. I yield myself to be led of You and to be a light and an example to them. I thank You that I am quick to hear, slow to speak and slow to anger, always radiating Your love to the children.

Reflection:

What strategies do I have in place to help me maintain composure?

_____

_____

_____

_____

_____

_____

_____

_____

_____

How attentively do I listen to my constituents, giving them a chance to express their concerns or disagreement?

_____

_____

_____

_____

_____

How can I make sure each one is treated fairly?

_____

_____

_____

_____

_____

_____

How am I building relationships or destroying their spirits?

_____

_____

_____

_____

_____

_____

_____

_____

_____

Day 8

Good Morning!
How Are You?

Scripture:

"Be sure to give each other a warm greeting. All of Christ's churches greet you."
~ Romans 16:16 (CEV)

When I became a principal, I developed the practice of greeting students as they entered the building. Every day, I would spend 30 to 40 minutes warmly waving good morning to the parents dropping students off and cordially greeting each student with words like: "Good Morning, John/Mary, How are you? ...So excited to see you this morning; glad you're here." And with a giant smile, I would give each one a huge hug or a pat on the head. Little did I know what positive affect this mere gesture was making, not only on students, but also on parents!

On mornings when my schedule prevented me from being there, they noticed, and upon my return, students trotted toward me with outstretched arms saying, "I missed you. Were you out of town?" Who would have thought such a simple gesture would have prompted such a caring response from them? The same technique can be effectively used by teachers when students enter the classroom doors. A kind word and a caring embrace are all it takes to set the stage for building relationships. It is how we make others feel that brings them back. It is in these small displays of kindness that students realize, "I am important enough for you to make intentional contact with me."

Prayer:

Heavenly Father,

Help me to be the gateway my students want to enter, and help them to see my classroom as a haven of peace and calmness in which they find love and acceptance.

Reflection:

Why do my students long to enter my classroom?

_____

_____

_____

_____

_____

_____

_____

What makes my classroom or office a welcoming space?

_____

_____

_____

_____

_____

_____

_____

_____

_____

Day 9

You Get An 'A'!

Scripture:

"For we are His workmanship, created in Christ Jesus for good works, which God prepared beforehand that we should walk in them."
~ Ephesians 2:10 (NKJV)

"And I thank Christ Jesus our Lord who has enabled me, because He counted me faithful, putting me into the ministry." ~ I Timothy 1:12 (NKJV)

During my rookie year of teaching, I presented a complex math concept with multiple steps to 13- and 14-year-old eighth graders. As I demonstrated an example on an overhead projector (which I know is pretty antiquated), a young man blurted out, "You're wrong. That's not right!"

Now I'm a degreed math teacher who knew what she was doing. And how dare he question my expertise! My first instinct was to retort with, "Let me show you how smart I am." But instead, I instructed him to please come to the front and share where I had faltered, and if his method were correct, he would receive an "A" for the class and would not have to do any work for the remainder of the quarter. Proudly strutting to the front, he proceeded to meticulously work the problem, artfully explaining each step as he went along the way. When he got to about the third step, he paused, sighing with a disappointing, "OH." Realizing his error, he exclaimed, "Never mind."

I celebrated his attempt, thanked him for showing initiative and quickly quieted his taunting classmates. I could have simply put him in his place and scolded him for talking without permission, but that was not the lesson of the day. The lesson was found in giving him voice and an opportunity to articulate his knowledge. Yes, I was technically right, but being right is not our mission. We are not here to show how smart we are but to aid them in discovering how smart they are.

Prayer:

Heavenly Father,

Help me to walk in humility with my students and to push them to uncover the greatest strengths on the inside of them. They are Your workmanship created in Christ for good works, which you have prepared for them to walk in. Thank You for trusting and gracing me for this great task.

Reflection:

How will I uncover the greatness hidden within my students?

_____

_____

_____

_____

_____

_____

_____

_____

_____

.

Day 10

Don't Worry – They Grow Up to Be Just Like You!

Scripture:

"A student is not superior to his teacher; but everyone, after he has been completely trained, will be like his teacher." ~ Luke 6:40 (AMP)

Math has always been my favorite subject because it just made sense to me. While shopping in the mall for sales, I got a kick out of calculating the final cost or determining the amount of change I would receive before the cashier figured it out on a machine. It gave me a rush. I met my match in the form of my ninth grade Algebra 1 teacher, Miss Frye.

Miss Frye was a great teacher who just took too long and used too many steps when solving problems. I often shared this observation with her. I'd say, "Miss Frye, you didn't need EIGHT steps to do that. It could have been completed in three." She'd respond, "Cheryl, I love the way you think, but you must show your work." Silently, I'd say in my head, "But that's pointless." It didn't take me long to realize that working problems my way, instead of hers, was causing my grades to reflect my brilliant shortcuts. I acquiesced after getting problems wrong for failing to show my work.

Fast forward eight years. I'm standing before an Algebra I class meticulously demonstrating and explaining all eight steps of my own Solve for the

Variable equation. A very bright student raises his hand and asks when acknowledged, "Why did you do all that? All you had to do was..." My response, "I love the way you think, but you must thoroughly show your work." My memory immediately took me back to my 1981 Algebra class with Miss Frye. I had become Miss Frye.

At 14, I thought Miss Frye was wasting my time. There were times when she allowed me to bring clarity to a concept for my classmates. But there were also times when my shortcuts got the best of me, and careless errors cost me precious points. She wasn't trying to kill my spirit, but instead she wanted to teach me the importance of processes and following instructions. Standing before my students, I realized I had the same responsibility to encourage my Smart Guy to continue seeing the other pathways but also to compel him to follow instructions and submit to using the process.

Prayer:

Heavenly Father,

I thank You for being our example. And as we continue to follow You as THE example and yield to Your guidance and direction, our students will reflect us as we reflect You. As Your word says they will follow us as we follow You. This is the teacher they are to become, Christ in the earth.

Reflection:

How do I demonstrate the teacher I want my students to become?

_____

_____

_____

_____

_____

_____

_____

_____

Which of my character traits should others not emulate? How will I allow God to adjust them?

_____

_____

_____

_____

_____

_____

Day 11

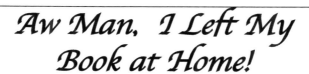

Aw Man, I Left My Book at Home!

Scripture:

As I conversed with a former student who now works at our school, he fondly recalled a memory from his days as a student in my Algebra 2 class. Apparently, one day, I had taken my textbook home and forgotten to bring it back to class. When I alerted the students of my dilemma, they were delighted assuming they would be math free, at least for that day. But in my very next breath, I said, "No worries." Then, I wrote on the board: "Don't worry! I don't need it!" And, I proceeded with the day's lesson.

While in my class, this same young man often made it a point to proclaim various teachers, "EDUCATORS" as if there was a distinction between an educator and a teacher. I think he was simply recognizing the fact that the craft of teaching ought to be respected. One has to understand that there is a distinction and believe that they owe this distinction to parents and students within the classroom environment. I think he was simply recognizing the craft of teaching was being demonstrated before him, and he respected that.

For more than 25 years, I taught at a private Christian school basically funded by tuition, but I also taught and tutored students at public institutions funded primarily by tax dollars. Regardless of the venue and source of funding, our students deserve our thorough preparation and our parents expect it. It is incumbent upon us to be good stewards of parents' investment into the lives of their children and to honor the call of our position to do so.

Prayer:

Heavenly Father,

I submit myself to You. Help me to be an EDUCATOR, one who respects the craft, my students, parents, my employer and most importantly You. This is my call, purpose and ministry. I am what I am because I have been equipped by You.

Reflection:

How do I illustrate my commitment to teaching?

_____

_____

_____

_____

_____

_____

_____

_____

_____

What are my students calling me?

_____

_____

_____

_____

_____

_____

_____

_____

_____

Day 12

Get Balanced!

Scripture:

"A false balance is abomination to the LORD: but a just weight is his delight." ~ Proverbs 11:1 (KJV)

My first year as a teacher was crowded with other "firsts." I graduated college in May, started a new teaching position in August, got married in September and found out I was pregnant in February. Whew! I get tired just remembering everything that took place within that short time span. Aside from it being my first year of teaching, it was also the year our Christian school began. Although I had no classroom experience and hadn't been trained to teach, I had majored in mathematics, the subject I would be teaching. Once hired, I attended several weeks of professional development in preparation for my new assignment.

Faced with such a great opportunity, I desperately wanted to do well. My desire to succeed pushed me head first into teaching and doing it well. It was a good thing that I wanted to do and give it my best, as students' educations were at stake. Nonetheless, I was also a newlywed since our wedding was just three weeks after school started. Although I was completely oblivious to the fact, somehow, my desire to be a good teacher had taken precedent over my responsibilities at home.

My failure to prioritize my family life set a negative foundation, and it took many years to fully grasp the impact that my excessive attention to school work was having on my home. Yes, I was called to teach, but I also made a vow to Mr. Riley. As we walk in our calling, we must be careful not to ruin our testimonies. Being everything to others at the expense of our families is not God's plan. It is imperative that we maintain proper balance between fulfilling our calling and living with those we love.

Prayer:

Heavenly Father,

Walking out Your purpose and plan for my life is my desire. I ask You to help me find the balance in my daily life and to maintain it in a way in which no area suffers. Give me wisdom and insight on how to manage all that I do. Enable me to strategically navigate my responsibilities to Your satisfaction, in Jesus' name. Amen.

Reflection:

What's tilting your scales?

_____

_____

_____

_____

_____

_____

_____

_____

_____

What adjustments are needed to bring my life into balance?

_____

_____

_____

_____

_____

_____

_____

Day 13

I Ain't Praying
for Them!

Scripture:

"*Through the* LORD*'s mercies we are not consumed, because His compassions fail not. They are new every morning; great is Your faithfulness.*"
~ *Lamentations 3:22-23 (NKJV)*

"For a just man falleth seven times, and riseth up again." ~ Proverbs 24:16 (KJV)

At the end of sixth period, I was mentally and spiritually exhausted, fed up. After the bell rang and the students in my eighth-grade Earth Science class departed, I collapsed in tears at my desk. They had been totally unruly, and I was done with them. I was ready to grab my purse and just leave, but my principal entered the room. Noticing my tears, he kneeled beside my desk and asked what was wrong. I spewed out, "These kids are bad! Their behavior was totally out of order. They're disrespectful, and I am not putting up with it any longer." Without a hint of alarm in his voice, he calmly and quietly responded, "You gotta' pray for them." I refrained from telling him what was on my mind, which was, "I don't wanna' pray for them! I'm done!"

He patiently shared with me the rocket science psychology behind the immature actions of children and their need to be trained, corrected, and loved…repeat. I knew all of that, but something was wrong with this group. After all, Christian children ought not act like that. Say "Amen," somebody. I wanted God to come down, sit beside me, give me a huge hug, rub my back and tell me He would beat every last one of them who had disrespected His favorite little teacher. But that didn't happen. Nor did I spend the next several hours in intercession praying for God to correct their actions, although, I definitely should have. On this day I received the revelation that children are children, regardless of what school they attend. All of them are "equal opportunity misbehavers." Realizing this, I came back the next day. Many times, all God wants is for us, to simply get back up and do it again. He has graced us to do everything He has called us to. Like a basketball player who has just been posterized in a dunk by his opponent, we must simply get up, shake it off and run the next play.

Prayer:

Heavenly Father,

Thank You for Your patience with me and all my shortcomings. Thank You for gracing me with the ability to be patient with students and to overlook their faults. I receive Your resilience. Help me not to take their actions personally and to love them through each challenge. Thank You for new beginnings each day, in Jesus' Name. Amen.

Reflection:

Recall an incident that pushed me to the limit? How did I handle it?

_____

_____

_____

_____

_____

_____

_____

What would I do differently?

_____

_____

_____

_____

_____

_____

Day 14

Give Us This Day
Our Daily Bread

Scripture:

It's Monday morning. Miss Davis walks into her creative writing class ready to deliver a lesson on journal writing. She has taught for years and could probably do it in her sleep. As she writes a sample entry on the board and begins explaining the lesson, several hands go up. "What's a journal entry?" "How long does it have to be?" "I don't have nothing to write about." Miss Davis responds to each student redirecting them to the lesson examples and instructions she had just outlined in PowerPoint. But the questions and comments keep coming, and Miss Davis gets irritated. "Follow the example," she exclaims. They respond "I still don't get it."

As professional educators, we've been vetted through the educational processes of our universities, certifications required by our states, as well as through the hiring procedures of our employers. We know what we're doing, and we have the goods to prove it. Wielding all the right credentials, we enter our classrooms ready to teach, because we know what to do. Knowing what to do and being confident in that knowledge is half of the battle. Yet, sometimes our expertise, as valuable as it is, can cause us to unconsciously lock God out. Class routines over time, can become as repetitious as a ticking clock; we fail to check in to see what changes God wants to make to our lesson plans. He has the necessary information, the course and direction we should take. But at times, we experts move presumptuously which results in the failure of our best prepared plans. We should practice checking in with God daily to make sure our lesson plans align with His.

Prayer:

Heavenly Father,

These are Your children. You've made them, and You know all about them. You are the source of all information and possess the solution to every question that has been and will be presented. I ask You to guide me through every lesson. I receive Your guidance and help, and I thank You that total understanding is a reality to each student sitting in this classroom. I thank You that their understanding is revealed through articulation and application, and each student demonstrates a full understanding of the information presented, in Jesus' Name. Amen.

Reflection:

What tasks am I trying to accomplish all by myself?

_____

_____

_____

_____

_____

_____

_____

What adjustments can I make to ensure God is a part of my daily lesson plans?

_____

_____

_____

_____

_____

_____

_____

Day 15

I Prayed and Asked God

Scripture:

"Call unto me, and I will answer thee, and show thee great and mighty things, which thou knowest not." ~ Jeremiah 33:3 (KJV)

"How will I reach this class, Lord? You know their reputation, their seemingly lack of interest in all things academic. They talk when the teacher is talking. Their grades and performances don't align with their abilities. They are capable of so much more. What can I do, God? How can I turn this around? I need Your help." – Ms. Jane Jones

Ms. Jones prayed this prayer for her Physical Science class. She needed God's help to reach and engage her students. After praying, God reminded her of a bridge building competition sponsored by her state's transportation department. She received the announcement several years before and had tucked it away, but somehow it resurfaced just in time for the event. She felt preparing for this off-site event could give her students the boost in confidence they needed.

The competition required a solid understanding of cause and effect, basic physics and math applications. These were topics the Physical Science class would normally explore. The competition was a compilation of class exercises designed to help students better understand the course requirements.

This event would help them connect the dots between model building and real-life situations. While not ecstatic about the project, Ms. Jones' class wanted to compete, present their findings and share their bridge in the oral presentation. After practicing in class, the students strategically built and presented their model which they explained by artfully performing an original rap song at the statewide competition. They received a standing ovation and encore requests from their competitors and contest judges. What an awesome experience! The students gained new knowledge, synchronized and articulated their understanding, received accolades for their performance and finished second in the competition. This is the purpose of education. Congratulations to Ms. Jones and her students! They rocked it!

Prayer:

Heavenly Father,
These are Your children. I am simply a steward. I know and understand the information required to move them to class mastery and completion. I submit my academic know-how to You. Guide me to the resources, activities and opportunities that will enable me to reach each individual who sits before me. I receive Your help in Jesus' Name. Amen.

Reflection:

Is there a class or student I need God's help with reaching? Describe the situation.

_____

_____

_____

_____

_____

_____

Share with God what I would like to see happen with my class.

_____

_____

_____

_____

_____

_____

Day 16

Won't He Do It?

Scripture:

"God is not a man, that he should lie; neither the son of man, that he should repent: hath he said, and shall he not do it? or hath he spoken, and shall he not make it good?" ~ Numbers 23:19 (KJV)

"Delight yourself also in the Lord: and He shall give you the desires of your heart."
~ Psalm 37:4 (NKJV)

Several years ago, I began my third attempt at obtaining my master's degree. I was in a student-friendly program that required me to attend class once a week for three hours and complete the remaining portions online via peer study groups. The program consisted of five consecutive semesters – fall, spring, summer, fall and spring again. In roughly 18 months, I could attain the degree that had taken over two decades to complete. Not only would I receive a master's but my principal's license as well.

While going through the program, I taught full time, tutored 10 to 15 hours a week and managed my family obligations. With all the demands, I began feeling stressed. As I got closer to graduation, my stress intensified to the point I felt mentally paralyzed, especially when I had to write papers or do a project. It was as if my brain had gone on vacation. I remember curling up on the sofa feeling completely overwhelmed with thoughts of coming up short and not achieving my goals. It seemed the closer I got to the finish line, the more challenging it became to meet my objectives.

For several weeks, thoughts of inadequacy surfaced whenever I had to complete course work. I shared my desperation with my husband and a few friends who encouraged me saying by I could do it. Jerking the slack out of me, one friend told me, "You got this! You are weeks away from your goal. Snap out of it and push to the finish line." She and another friend prayed me through. After I prayed, God led me to resources I needed. I had been internalizing my workload when I should have been casting every care upon Him.

Although my 20-year quest was coming to an end, the finish line was in sight, despite the fact I had been temporarily sidetracked by a lack of focus. I began to thank God for all that had taken place. I was reminded of lyrics in the Old James Cleveland song, "*I Don't Feel No Ways Tired.*" My faithful God had not brought me this far to leave me; He would see me through. My belief and confidence in Him put me over. I made it, completed all assignments and graduated with honors! Won't He Do It!

Prayer:

Heavenly Father,

You are a faithful God. You don't change! You watch over Your Word to perform it. Thank you for Your faithfulness. Thank you for your commitment to fulfill Your Word in my life. I can trust You and Your love for me, and I choose to rest in it in Jesus' Name. Amen

Reflection:

What is one thing I am believing God for?

_____

_____

_____

_____

_____

How will I demonstrate my trust in Him to do it?

_____

_____

_____

_____

_____

_____

Day 17

Who Am I Not to Be?

Scripture:

"God has not given us a spirit of fear but of power, and of love and of a sound mind."
~ 2 Timothy 1:7 (NKJV)

"And ye shall know the truth, and the truth shall make you free." ~ John 8:32 (KJV)

"Our deepest fear is not that we are inadequate. Our deepest fear is that we are powerful beyond measure. It is our light, not our darkness that most frightens us. We ask ourselves, 'Who am I to be brilliant, gorgeous, talented, fabulous?' Actually, who are you not to be? You are a child of God. Your playing small does not serve the world. There is nothing enlightened about shrinking so that other people won't feel insecure around you. We are all meant to shine, as children do. We were born to make manifest the glory of God that is within us. It's not just in some of us; it's in everyone. And as we let our own light shine, we unconsciously give other people permission to do the same. As we are liberated from our own fear, our presence automatically liberates others." — __Marianne Williamson__, __A Return to Love: Reflections on the Principles of "A Course in Miracles"__

I recently read an article on Flipped Learning. Flipped Learning is a teaching strategy in which an instructor assigns his or her class to view videos via mediums like Khan Academy or the instructor's

70

personal library prior to the teacher presenting the information. The goal is to provide the necessary background information in a setting where students can learn at their own pace. Students have the option of fast forwarding and rewinding based on their level of understanding and mastery. Once viewed, students enter the classroom with baseline knowledge that now provides a platform for the teacher to create an active learning environment where students can apply the knowledge gained. This allows the teacher to move about the class assessing individual knowledge and shedding light on areas of concern. It's an awesome concept.

The author of the article also pointed out why teachers are reluctant to share information from their libraries. Among the reasons given were they fear the judgmental responses of others. Isn't it interesting that regardless of age, we all want to be accepted and affirmed? We want to know that what we do is good enough. Apprehension caused by the need for affirmation prompts many to isolate themselves in a vacuum. But great things are happening in every classroom, and we need to share them with our peers.

We accomplish this through peer observations. As educators observe one another, they get a firsthand glimpse of the glowing attributes that work for others and can celebrate and imitate them. On the other hand, observations are just as helpful in identifying areas for growth opportunities where improvement is needed. We all have strategies that others can benefit from, and there are work habits that we can learn from others. In order to improve our skills, we must accept critiques as well as compliments.

Everyone has something they do best, and it is imperative we identify that strength and have the courage to share it to help others reach their fullest potential. Isn't this what we tell our children?

Prayer:

Heavenly Father,

Help me to value and appreciate the skill sets and wisdom of my peers and to eagerly and humbly accept their feedback. Even if an evaluation appears too harsh or insignificant, I ask You to help me remain gracious and unoffended, so I can listen attentively and make changes that will strengthen my students, my character and my skills. I thank You for it, in Jesus' name. Amen.

Reflection:

What is my area of expertise? Best lesson?

_____

_____

_____

How can I share this with others to improve their teaching practices?

Day 18

Your Word Is Your Bond

Scripture:

Work hard so you can present yourself to God and receive his approval. Be a good worker, one who does not need to be ashamed and who correctly explains the word of truth. ~ 2 Timothy 2:15 (NLT)

Setting aside time to assist your children with homework is a common occurrence. They go to school, gain new insight, complete classwork, discuss information shared, then receive homework assignments to practice and test knowledge retained. The child returns home and heads to the designated area, to do homework. After hitting a roadblock, the child request your help. No worries. With a high school diploma and a college degree, you know you are equipped to help your child. So, with all your confidence you begin, "Sure sweetie, what's your question?"

That was a typical response to my youngest son while he was in the second grade. Periodically, he'd ask math questions, and up until then, he had eagerly accepted my answers. I mean I had been through the second grade, right? So, I've got this, as a math major, this was my thing. Explaining the new math concepts he was learning would be a breeze. But after I had confidently given him my expert explanation of the concept, he responds, "That's not how Mrs. Smith did it." So I go through the proper mathematical steps again only to get the same response from him. Since he often shared the wonderful things that went on in her classroom, I knew my son and Mrs. Smith had a special relationship, and I appreciated that. All parents want their children to have positive relationships with their teachers. As I assisted my son, I continued getting the same doubtful reply from him throughout the school year until finally, I picked up the phone one night and called Mrs. Smith. I said to her, "If I hear your name one more time, I'm going to pack my son's clothes and move him in with you because he does not accept my explanations." We both laughed.

That incident prompted me to take note of the power of our influence as teachers and the plausibility of what we say and do. Our students take what we say as gospel. And that's a good thing provided we are teaching them accurately. Knowing and honoring the power of our influence is a responsibility we must never take lightly. We are life impactors, and what we do will live well beyond the 10 months students spend in our classrooms.

Prayer:

Heavenly Father,

Thank You for trusting me with Your children. It is a pleasure to serve You. I submit myself to Your direction. I pray that my words are Your words and my thoughts are Your thoughts. Help me to consistently provide accurate information to my students that will point them toward their destiny in You.

Reflection:

What life-impacting examples have I displayed as a teacher?

_____

_____

_____

_____

_____

What responses have I heard from students? Discuss your thoughts.

_____

_____

_____

_____

_____

_____

Day 19

I Won't Quit

Scripture:

"I had fainted, unless I had believed to see the goodness of the LORD in the land of the living. Wait on the LORD: be of good courage, and he shall strengthen thine heart: wait, I say, on the LORD."

~ Psalms 27:13-14 (KJV)

Life circumstances sometimes paint a discouraging picture, and the picture shows us the facts. While facts may be true, they are not *the truth.* For 15 years, Arthur Boorman lived with the fact that he was a disabled veteran. Serving as a paratrooper in the Gulf War had taken a toll on his legs and back, and as a result, Arthur gained quite a bit of weight and required crutches to assist him with walking.

After perusing the internet, Arthur came across an article on Diamond Dallas Page (DDP) Yoga. Because of the nature of his injuries, he could not participate in high-impact exercises. So, he reached out to the exercise creator who encouraged him and agreed to support him in his quest to lose weight, walk again and find relief from his pain. Neither knew what the outcome would be when they started. As Arthur slowly began his journey, the pair communicated via phone and email.

With Dallas' encouragement, Arthur kept pushing and remained persistent; though he fell many times, he didn't quit. He gradually got stronger and lost weight in the process. The specialized techniques of DDP produced great balance and flexibility which gave him hope that walking again was indeed possible. After only 10 months, Arthur lost 140 pounds and was not just walking but running.

Arthur's story is inspiring and hopeful, especially since he had been told for years what he would not be able to do. But he never gave up hope of seeing his dream realized. As he kept seeking and pressing forward, he made the connection with Dallas who not only empathized with him but was moved to join him in the fray. There are times when we all need someone to help pull us through and to believe with us that we can indeed reach our desired goals.

Today's scripture is one of my favorites. All of God's Word is good, but in this passage, I find solace in the fact that no matter how dark or difficult a situation is, light will dispel the darkness if we don't let go of our hope. The fact is Arthur's persistence uncovered what would become his truth.

Prayer:

Heavenly Father,

Thank You for the hope that Your word provides. It reminds me that You are always with me and will never leave me alone. I believe that whatever I go through You will get me through. Thank You for being with me and giving me the daily strength not to quit.

Reflection:

What am I pressing through?

_____

_____

_____

_____

_____

What resources or individuals can support me in the process?

_____

_____

_____

_____

_____

Day 20

Be Consistent

Scripture:

"Jesus Christ the same yesterday, and today, and forever." ~ Hebrews 13:8 (KJV)

"For I am the LORD, I change not; therefore ye sons of Jacob are not consumed." ~ Malachi 3:6 (KJV)

My husband has worked or consulted in the retail industry since he was 15 years old. As a consultant, he often advises his clients on best practices in the area of customer service. During a recent presentation, he began with a warm-up discussion on customer experience at top-rated stores. The conversation began with one of the participants stating that whenever she has a bad day, she goes to Publix because their staff is so inviting and ready to serve and assist customers in any way. Others echoed similar sentiments.

Nordstrom department store was given great reviews by all the audience members, except one individual who refuted claims about their excellent customer service. My husband asked her to expound. She said on a visit to the store, the clerks weren't as accommodating. No one was available to assist her in the department, and when she asked for help, a clerk told her he worked in a different department but would find someone to assist her. He never returned, nor did anyone else. By the time she was ready to pay for her items, checkout lines were long. My husband then asked, "How often have you had that type of experience at Nordstrom?" Her response was "Once."

Schools, shops and businesses may have enjoyed reputations from stellar performances for years, but all it takes is one isolated incident to turn the tables and change a company's trajectory. It is imperative that we consistently maintain our reputation corporately and individually. It is what we do repeatedly that establishes who we are. If we want customers to remain loyal, we must habitually demonstrate and set standards that reflect our desired message. Our reputation stems from our public image, and it must be upheld by everyone in our organization.

Heavenly Father,

It is our wish to daily demonstrate the standards and statues that make us who we are. We thank You for showing us how to take advantage of opportunities to uphold our name and to daily walk in excellence in all we do. We thank You for giving us insight on how we can best serve those we work for and how to display examples of faithfulness in our professions. We receive Your help and we are the better for it in Jesus' name. Amen.

Reflection:

How am I aligning with my business' mission and purpose?

_____

_____

_____

_____

_____

How can faithfulness be displayed in the

workplace?

_____

_____

_____

_____

_____

Day 21

So, Where's Deborah?

Scripture:

"And if ye have not been faithful in that which is another man's, who shall give you that which is your own?" ~ Luke 16:12 (KJV)

"And whatsoever ye do, do it heartily, as to the Lord, and not unto men." ~ Colossians 3:23 (KJV)

For more than 20 years, I have served as a workshop facilitator in various arenas. My journey began in the early 90's when I became an independent training consultant for a local company that operated throughout the southeast. When I first ventured out, attendees would often inquire about where the regular facilitator was. I would hear, "Where is she?" "Who are you?" "How long have you been training?" "Are you as good as she is?"

These questions were quite intimidating. What had I gotten myself into? Now I understood where they were coming from; the owner of the business was an excellent facilitator. She had a larger than life personality and delivery. The participants came with valid expectations, and they were not expecting little ole' me.

In those days, since I traveled alone, I registered participants, presented the workshops and sold company materials. There was no one around with whom to share my concerns or invite to my pity party. I was it, and it was incumbent upon me to produce.

In case you're wondering, here's how I handled the situation. First, I went to the restroom, because anxiety had kicked in. Then I began talking to myself, saying... "You do this every day. In fact, that's how you got here. The owner, the very one they wanted to hear, has assigned you. She trusts you. You can do this. You ARE a teacher. Go be what you have been called to be." Next, I reminded myself that I had studied and prepared for this presentation. I then began a continual dialogue with my Father, God. I reminded Him and myself that He had not given me a spirit of fear, but of power, of love and of a sound mind (2 Timothy 1:7).

I began to pray, "God, as I walk down this aisle and speak to these people, I ask you to speak to them through me. Cause each participant to receive exactly what they need. I yield my time and talents to You. Direct my path, guide the presentation, order each point and bring clarity, understanding and reproducibility. Let each participant recognize that they've been equipped to take the information back to their company and immediately implement it."

Well, He did just that. No, I didn't sing to them. ☺ But with each point, I was able to provide real-world examples, along with research-based information and best practices. The audience was engaged and entertained and verbally said so. The workshop surveys confirmed their satisfaction as well. I was so grateful to God and humbled that He hears and answers my prayers.

God wants to make our names great because this points others to Him. As we properly represent our employers, we are ultimately representing our God. As we purpose to give and do our best, we are living epistles for Him.

Prayer:

Heavenly Father,

My desire is to please You in all that I do. I believe by doing so, those I serve are also pleased. Thank You for showing me exactly how to do that as I perform my daily tasks. I choose to glorify You in all I do.

Reflection:

What are others saying about my faithfulness in the workplace? What adjustments can I make to improve in this area?

_____

_____

_____

_____

_____

_____

Day 22

I Am the Absolute Best At What I Do!

Scripture:

"The LORD will make you the head (leader) and not the tail (follower); and you will be above only, and you will not be beneath, if you listen and pay attention to the commandments of the LORD your God, which I am commanding you today, to observe them carefully." ~ Deuteronomy 28:13 (AMP)

The scripture above is a declaration made by a first-year teacher. I had known this individual for over a decade. He had been called into the ministry at age 12 and preached his first sermon shortly thereafter. He was a dynamic preacher even then. The fact he had come from a family of godly men and women who served as his examples may have contributed to his success. His oratorical skills led him to join his high school Mock Trial team where he would repeatedly receive Best Witness and Best Attorney honors over the course of four years.

Professionals in the field would often compliment his talents and seal their comments with offers of internships and positions at their practices. This talented individual had aspirations for both the legal and medical industries. He graduated high school with honors, received his Bachelor of Science degree from a prestigious university and moved on to graduate school where he pursued his law interest.

Then he decided to teach for a while and began his tenure confessing Deuteronomy 28:13 and instilling a spirit of excellence in his students. He has produced highly acclaimed Mock Trial teams who have been honored with Best Attorney and Best Witness awards. Also, he is an advisor to our school's award-winning Rocket Team.

It all began with his profound scriptural declaration. He set the stage for his success by determining his expectations. Then he shaped his world with words from his own mouth, and so should we.

Prayer:

Heavenly Father,

Help me to speak words that will lead me to my intended destination. I thank You that my words will establish, build and propel me to the predestined place for me. I am who You say I am and I can do what You say I can do in Jesus' name. Amen.

Reflection:

What are my daily confessions?

_____

_____

_____

_____

_____

_____

What kind of results are my confessions yielding?

_____

_____

_____

_____

What *statements am I making about myself?*

_____

_____

_____

_____

_____

How does this align with the way I wish to be viewed/represented?

_____

_____

_____

_____

_____

Day 23

I Will Pray!

Scripture:

"Rejoice always, pray without ceasing, give thanks in all circumstances; for this is the will of God in Christ Jesus for you."
~ *1 Thessalonians 5:16-18 (NIV)*

"For My thoughts are not your thoughts, nor are your ways My ways," says the LORD. For as the heavens are higher than the earth, so are My ways higher than your ways, and My thoughts than your thoughts. "For as the rain comes down, and the snow from heaven, and do not return there, but water the earth, and make it bring forth and bud, that it may give seed to the sower and bread to the eater, so shall My word be that goes forth from My mouth; it shall not return to Me void, but it shall accomplish what I please, and it shall prosper in the thing for which I sent it." ~ Isaiah 55:8-11 (NKJV)

Prayer is about relationship and connection. In our daily walk we hold various positions – spouse, parent, coworker, friend, etc. As we transition to each, we maintain these roles through daily communications. These interactions begin with a small salutation of some sort each day. "Good Morning, Honey." "Hello, Sunshine." "Hi Bill, How was your weekend?" The exchange is usually followed by some sort of conversation, strategy, plan or update. Once completed, we move to execution based upon the outcome. As a parent, this could involve identifying your child's schedule for the day, lunch preparation, drop-off, pick-up and afterschool activities. A similar conversation would go on with Bill at the office as he and coworkers discuss the day's deliverables and expectations.

Just as we routinely connect with those around us in order to carry out daily tasks, the same is required in our relationship with God. He knows what lies ahead, and He has a plan for getting us through it all. As Isaiah 55:8 tells us, "His thoughts are not our thoughts, nor are His ways our ways." The All-Knowing One has the insight and the instructions I need to get through my day. He has insight about my marriage, my job and my children.

As I commune with Him, I can obtain instructions on what the day's game plan should be. When we fail to communicate with those in our circle, chaos can ensue. Failure to obtain the details of the day can cause things to slip through the cracks. It's funny how we understand this on the human level, yet frequently miss it on the God level. He wants to provide the necessary strategies and needed information, but we must initiate that contact with Him. The Word of God is full of examples of individuals who sought God, and He answered them. He encourages us to call upon Him and He will answer us too.

Prayer:

Heavenly Father,

Thank You, for being there waiting to commune with me. Forgive me for the times when I didn't prioritize my time with You. I enjoy our time together and I recommit Myself to daily connecting with you in Jesus' name. Amen.

Reflection:

How can I adjust my schedule, so that I spend more time with God?

_____

_____

_____

_____

_____

_____

_____

_____

_____

_____

Day 24

Check Your Playlist

Scripture:

"Finally, brethren, whatsoever things are true, whatsoever things are honest, whatsoever things are just, whatsoever things are pure, whatsoever things are lovely, whatsoever things are of good report; if there be any virtue, and if there be any praise, think on these things." ~ Philippians 4:8 (KJV)

Several Months ago, I was involved in a six-car accident in which my vehicle was totaled. Every airbag deployed, and the entire left side was completely crushed after my car collided with a car sitting diagonally in the middle of the highway. That caused my two left wheels to be hurled across the concrete median. As the collision occurred, I remember gripping the steering wheel and when it was all over, saying, "God You Are Amazing!"

I leave for work between 4:45 and 5:15 a.m. to dodge the morning traffic and get a jumpstart on the day's agenda. While en route, I listen to sermons on CD, or some portion of the Word. On this particular morning, I was listening to healing scriptures set to music. When it was all over, *Psalm 34:20* was playing on my speakers: *"He keepeth all his bones: not one of them is broken."* I was floored by the timing. Based on the condition of the vehicles, it was a miracle that no life was lost. I was able to climb out of the passenger side of my car with assistance. God had preserved me and He was reminding me through that scripture that He was there in the midst. What a Mighty God He is!

On the day of the accident, my playlist was made up of healing scriptures. At times, I listen to recorded confessions produced by me or someone else, and at other times, I may play Word CD's of messages. This practice has been a blessing as it helps shape and set the tone for my day. We get to determine the atmosphere in which we live, and we can create it our atmosphere by what we intentionally put in or let into our spirits through our ears.

When that accident occurred, I was fear free and didn't wonder about what would happen; instead, I held onto the steering wheel as my angels moved me to safety. I am so grateful for the peace that God's Word provides.

Prayer:

Heavenly Father,

I am so grateful for the peace I found during my time in the Word. I can rest knowing that You are watching over Your Word to perform it. It does not return to You void, and it accomplishes that which You please (Isaiah 55:11). Your Word is true for me and for my life. Thank you, Father. I trust You, and I trust Your word. In Jesus' name. Amen.

Reflection:

What do I listen to while preparing for work and while traveling to and from work?

_____

_____

_____

_____

_____

_____

_____

_____

_____

_____

_____

_____

Day 25

Our Words Have Power

Scripture:

"Let the words of my mouth, and the meditation of my heart, be acceptable in thy sight, O LORD, my strength, and my redeemer." ~ Psalm 19:14 (KJV)

My great-grandmother used to sing this psalm. I loved the song and often taught it to my students. As I grew older, I realized what the writer was asking and the responsibility that went with the request.

Years later, I began teaching this to my students using an object lesson to bring it home. The lesson began with a large piece of chart paper with a stick drawing of a boy. I called him my friend, Buddy. I would begin the lesson introducing Buddy as a new student in our school. The lesson would continue with me asking the children to make statements about Buddy. As negative statements were made, the students were to come up and deface the picture of Buddy by punching it, balling up the paper, or marking it up. After a few rounds, we would discuss how Buddy looked and how he might feel. We might then ask if anyone in the group had encountered a similar experience. Then we might ask if anything could be done to help Buddy, and what had helped them.

The students shared how they could apologize and follow the apology up with kind words and caring touches. This time students would come to the front with positive confessions coupled with soothing gestures. They pressed the wrinkles with their hands, taped the cuts and erased the marks they had drawn. We then paused, looked at Buddy and asked how this affected him. The students realized that though the wounds had been dressed, there was still evidence of them. The apology was needed and so was the mending, but they didn't completely heal him.

We were then able to discuss the affect words have on us and how they must be carefully selected. We want to please God in what we say and do. We want to build up our friends and loved ones and not tear them down. Words can be like punches, so we want to make sure our words spread love and build bridges rather than hate and division.

Prayer:

Heavenly Father,

Help me to speak words that build and grow others. I will speak words that point them to You. Forgive me for those times that I have spoken too quickly and caused injury. I denounce those words, and I come against their negative effects. Heal the hearts and wounds of those impacted. I yield my tongue to You, and I commit to aligning my words with Yours in Jesus' name. Amen.

Reflections:

How have I been impacted by words spoken about me?

_____

_____

_____

_____

_____

_____

How can I adjust my conversation?

_____

_____

_____

_____

_____

_____

_____

_____

Day 26

They Trust Us

Scripture:

"The trustworthy person will get a rich reward, but a person who wants quick riches will get into trouble.
~ Proverbs 28:20 (NLT)

"He who is faithful in a very little thing is faithful also in much; and he who is unrighteous in a very little thing is unrighteous also in much. Therefore if you have not been faithful in the use of unrighteous wealth, who will entrust the true riches to you? And if you have not been faithful in the use of that which is another's, who will give you that which is your own?" ~ Luke 16:10-12 (NASB)

The great educator Marva Collins is one of my heroes of the classroom. This phenomenal woman had a heart for children and a desire to see them operate at the apex of their capabilities. She illustrated this characteristic by opening her own school after being told by an administrator to stop caring so much for her students. "Close the door, realize that not all of them are capable of achieving, just do what you can and move on."

The purpose of the Westside Preparatory School was to disprove the myth that schools are better off leaving behind students who do not learn quickly enough. Mrs. Collins said, "All children can learn if they are not taught too thoroughly that they cannot learn," and she would work to that end. Word spread and parents began to seek out Mrs. Collins and enroll their children in Westside Preparatory. Parents appreciated the mission and quickly saw her commitment to the students and her desire for them to achieve. It was not uncommon for her to assist students with developmental delays, or behavior concerns. Mrs. Collins took great care to meet the needs of each child. She set standards and challenged them to perform accordingly. Students who were once seen as underachievers went on to become doctors and lawyers and to speak before presidents.

Years later, these students would come back to appreciate and celebrate her commitment to them and their progress. Parents were often brought to tears as they witnessed the negative diagnoses of professionals being dispelled in the lives of their children. They trusted her heart, and she did not let them down.

The Marva Collins story has served as fuel for me throughout my years in education. She saw potential, not problems; hope, not despair. She is an excellent example of miracles in the classroom and the fulfillment of the impossible.

Prayer:

Heavenly Father,

Thank You for calling me to this position called teaching. Thank You for equipping me with the tools to perform the tasks set before me. This can only be done with Your grace and in Your strength, Thank You for both. I commit myself to the call and the daily responsibility of walking it out. In Jesus' name. Amen.

Reflection:

What habits illustrate my trustworthiness?

_____

_____

_____

_____

_____

_____

_____

_____

_____

Day 27

Parents As Partners

Scripture:

"Can two walk together, except they be agreed?"
~ *Amos 3:3*

*"Train up a child in the way he should go: and when
he is old, he will not depart from it."*
~ *Proverbs 22:6 (KJV)*

Establishing a solid school-home connection at
the beginning of the school year is a necessity.
Parents want to know that the person assigned to
their child has their best interest at heart. Parents
want to know they can safely trust them to care for
their whole being. I recently had a conversation with
a parent who had moved to a new state. Both parents
were starting new positions, and their children were
starting at new schools.

The family had two sons, one in middle school
and the other elementary. They had toured the school
the previous school year and were pleased with what
they saw. But by the time they arrived, the school had
experienced several personnel shifts. Although the
elementary teacher they had previously met had not
returned, they proceeded with enrollment. But just
three weeks into the semester, their young son did

not want to return to school and cried at the thought of having to go.

The child was also struggling to understand mathematics problems. When the parent brought the concerns to the teacher, she replied, the young man needed to adjust to her teaching style, and if additional time was required, it was available at a rate of $40 dollars per hour. Both the parent and the child were perplexed. The mother, also an educator, was out done by the response and immediately began searching for a new school.

In order for students to blossom and grow, they need a solid support system. They need individuals who will rally behind them, assist in their development and build bridges to solutions.

I choose to believe that the teacher in this story meant no harm to the parent or the child, but it is vitally important that a workable agreement is made between all parties. Parents, students, teachers and administrators each have roles and must perform their duties in order for the team to function properly. We are a team, and the team is only victorious when all members do their part.

Prayer:

Heavenly Father,

Thank You for a spirit of agreement existing between our teachers and parents. I thank You that we each share the common goal of developing young people who will live out their lives serving and honoring You. Guide each of us, so that we can properly guide Your children. Help us to train them according to the call You have for their lives. In Jesus' name. Amen

Reflection:

How can I team up with parents to meet my students' needs?

_____

_____

_____

_____

_____

_____

_____

_____

_____

Day 28

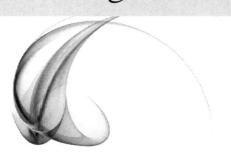

Called to What...
Service?

Scripture:

"I therefore, the prisoner of the Lord, beseech you that ye walk worthy of the vocation wherewith ye are called, with all lowliness and meekness, with longsuffering, forbearing one another in love; endeavouring to keep the unity of the Spirit in the bond of peace." ~ Ephesians 4:1-3 (KJV)

Teaching is a calling. We are often called public servants. Teaching is the one profession that grooms students for all other professions. Teachers go to great lengths to insure students are ready to move from one level to the next. Children come to us as empty vessels in need of filling. Our mission, once a need has been identified, is to address it. As I look back over my years in the classroom, I remember the horror stories about students' negative experiences with math. Many viewed math as a hurdle they could not overcome. I encountered this during my very first year of teaching Algebra 1. One young lady in the class just did not get it and was unable to articulate what she didn't understand. When facing this dilemma, teachers often ask, "What don't you understand?" The child responds, "None of it."

This cycle can continue, going absolutely nowhere. From my experience with another student, I learned pupils don't always know what they don't understand. It is then that I must start at the beginning. We spent time going back to the very basics to establish foundational concepts to increase students' understanding. We set aside time prior to and after school, when necessary, to work with that young lady until she was able to solve problems independently.

The extra tasks are performed with the needs of the student in the forefront. The sooner disconnects can be addressed, the better it is for the student and the teacher. That way, we can setup strategies students can use, not only in the current course, but in those to follow. That young lady was able to grasp the content and went on to complete Algebra 1 and three additional math courses required for graduation. After graduation, she entered college, majored in nursing and has worked in the field for over 10 years.

My thoughts take me to another student who would stay late for tutoring and would even come to my home for sessions. She actually had a mental block when it came to math. Years later, she majored in mathematics, entered a teaching program and was named Mathematics Teacher of the Year during her first year. She replaced me when I transitioned to an administrative position. All things are indeed possible, and everyone can understand and articulate knowledge to others.

Prayer:

Heavenly Father,

Give me a heart of service toward my students. Allow Your love and compassion to flow through me to them. Give me the insight and wisdom to see their needs and the solutions to bring understanding to each of them. In Jesus' name, I thank You.

Reflections:

Do my students see me as a source of help in their times of need? What evidence supports my answer?

_____

_____

_____

_____

If not, how will you adjust?

_____

_____

_____

_____

Day 29

Always Growing

Scripture:

"Be diligent in these matters; give yourself wholly to them, so that everyone may see your progress."
~ *1 Timothy 4:15 (NIV)*

"Being confident of this, that he who began a good work in you will carry it on to completion until the day of Christ Jesus." ~ Philippians 1:6 (NIV)

My teaching career began in the late eighties during the days of the overhead projector and nice neat orderly rows of desks and chairs. But order did not always equate to learning or growth. While it worked for some, others got lost in the compliance process back then, just as many do now. Realizing that self-development is key to improvement, I understand the need to improve in every area. If we routinely require individuals to attend forums for professional development, this is par for the course. But growth must occur holistically.

Recognizing that we are three-part beings, spirit, soul and body, we must intentionally focus on each part individually, as all three parts are codependent. If you speak to your doctor, he would encourage you to get adequate rest, exercise three to five times per week, drink the appropriate amount of water, reduce your sugar intake and increase the amounts of fruits and vegetables you consume. In a conversation with your church leader, you may be advised to spend time communicating with God in prayer and worship, read your Bible and associate with like-minded people who will motivate and build you up. Neither area can be ignored, if we want to enjoy balanced growth.

I am a confessed workshop junkie. I love learning and discovering ways to improve my teaching practice. Seeing new methods and how they can assist me in reaching my students gives me a rush. It is not uncommon for me to spend time surfing the internet or reading a book on the latest educational research book or article.

Attending various learning events and then meshing them with tried and true techniques makes me a better educator. But if I don't couple it with the Word of God and a need to be led by Him, I have done a disservice to my students. I have to address their whole being, spirit, soul and body, just as I address mine. We are not complete if all parts are not pruned and fed.

Prayer:

Heavenly Father,

Just as You are a triune Being, so are we, and all three areas must be ministered to. Help us to give proper attention to our spirit, soul and body, so that we might be examples of You on earth. We want to be more and more like You.

Reflections:

List the growth habits I have in place to improve my spirit, soul and body.

_____

_____

_____

_____

_____

Which areas need to be pruned or enhanced in order for me to grow.

_____

_____

_____

_____

Day 30

We Want the Same Thing... Win-Win

Scripture:

"But thanks be to God! He gives us the victory through our Lord Jesus Christ."
~ 1 Corinthians 15:57 (NIV)

Over the years, I have sat in on parent conferences with teachers and have had one-on-one meetings with parents. Throughout these exchanges, it is important to note that the majority of parents come to conferences to gain insight on how they might best support the school's program. They're interested in knowing what role they can play in improving their child's performance.

While I sat in on a conference with a teacher, the parent addressed accusations of misbehavior and favoritism. The teacher attempted to respond to the parent's concern by recounting situations as they occurred in the classroom. Words were exchanged and before I knew it, the parent was standing and pointing across the table. It had turned into a "you-said-and-did" versus "the-student-said-and-did" disagreement. I quickly diffused the situation and assured the parent that she and the teacher had the same goal.

I have learned that listening and seeking to understand is far more profitable than getting your words heard. We began the conference again with my asking the parent what her concerns were. I repeated the concerns and then had the teacher to address them one by one. Once the parent was sufficiently satisfied, we brought the child into the meeting, assuring him that he was not in trouble. We advised him that we simply needed to understand his interpretation of the events, so we could determine what measures were needed to bring about a positive resolution. We then discussed the matter from his perspective, and the teacher addressed his concerns as well. We devised a plan for moving forward, so that everyone was on the same page and able to productively work together. I have found that involving students in this process creates a community and eliminates the attitude of, "Imma tell my momma on you."

Prayer:

Heavenly Father,

It is our desire to have healthy interactions with all stakeholders. Thank You for helping us to develop win-win situations between school personnel and our parents. We are all on the same team, fighting the same fight. Thank You for peaceful resolutions every time in Jesus' name. Amen.

Reflection:

As God helps me to see solutions and not challenges, what steps can I take to quickly diffuse negative situations and resolve conflicts?

_____

_____

_____

_____

_____

_____

_____

_____

_____

Day 31

Staying in My Lane

Scripture:

"But, speaking the truth in love, may grow up in all things into Him who is the head – Christ – from whom the whole body, joined and knit together by what every joint supplies, according to the effective working by which every part does its share, causes growth of the body for the edifying of itself in love."
~ *Ephesians 4:15-16 (NKJV)*

For You formed my inward parts; You covered me in my mother's womb. I will praise You, for I am fearfully and wonderfully made; Marvelous are Your works, and that my soul knows very well.
~ *Psalms 139:13-14 (NKJV)*

Often during my days in the classroom, one of my colleagues would comment on how she would pray with students for healing or share scriptures with them for receiving salvation; yet, those students didn't receive healings manifested or commit their lives to Christ until they arrived in my classroom. It became a running joke between us around the question, "God, how could you allow her to reap the fruit when I planted the seed?" According to 1 Corinthians 3:6, some plant, some water, but God gives the increase. In other words, we all have a distinct role to play.

We must avoid comparing ourselves to others and desiring to have what they have and do what they do. Each of us has been uniquely crafted and anointed for our very own specific calling. Comparing ourselves with others devalues our calling. As a 30-year mathematics instructor, I love math, and my desire has been to teach it well. Since God knew that, He did not place me in an English department which would have been an epic failure. Although I endeavor to be an excellent teacher, whenever I write anything, you can rest assured there is a dictionary, grammar correction tool or an editor/proofreader nearby. Otherwise, my outcome could be dreadful. I actually hate writing papers. Yet, I have never been jealous or envious of English instructors, and I don't wish to fulfill their roles. Instead, I celebrate their gifts and pray for them often. I want them to be the very best readers, writers, editors and vocabulary enhancers they can be.

If any of us shows up to teach in the wrong room with the wrong content, those we minister to will suffer. Our presence there would be as out of place as my ear being attached to my heel. Any misalignment would prevent the organ from functioning properly. That's what happens when we waste time wishing we were someone else or attempting to play someone else's position. Instead, let's celebrate others! God has chosen you for YOUR gifts! Bloom where you are planted! You have a beautiful garden. Plant, water and cultivate it, and it will yield your intended harvest.

Prayer:

Heavenly Father,

Thank You for taking the time to uniquely craft me for my specific calling. With Your help, I will strive to honor it by giving You and those I serve my very best. It is my heart's desire to constantly seek You as I walk out the plan and prepare myself spiritually, academically, socially and professionally to properly represent You and the students in all that I do. In Jesus' name, I thank you. Amen.

Reflection:

What is my call and what value does it bring to others?

_____

_____

_____

_____

_____

_____

_____

_____

_____

_____

_____

_____

How can I honor God and celebrate my anointing?

_____

_____

_____

_____

_____

_____

_____

_____

_____

Are YOU Devoted to Serve?

ORDER YOUR COPIES NOW!

Website: www.CherylCRiley.com

Facebook/ Devoted to Him for Them

amazon.com

59612063R00080

Made in the USA
Columbia, SC
06 June 2019